Windows 10:

2021 Complete User Guide. Everything You Need to Know Before Getting Started with Windows 10. Information About October 2020 Update Included.

ISBN: 9798703274439

CONTENTS

Chapter 1: Installing and Downloading Windows 10 on your Computer.

Download Windows 10 Disc Image (ISO File) - Microsoft
https://www.microsoft.com/software-download/windows10 ▼
You can use this page to **download** a disc image (**ISO** file) that can be used to install or reinstall
Windows 10. The image can also be used to create installation ...

This chapter is for those who have not upgraded to Windows 10. If you are already using an operating system, follow the next chapter.

If you are currently using Windows 7 or Windows 8 and can update using Windows Update you can upgrade to Windows 10. Please enable the Windows Update service.

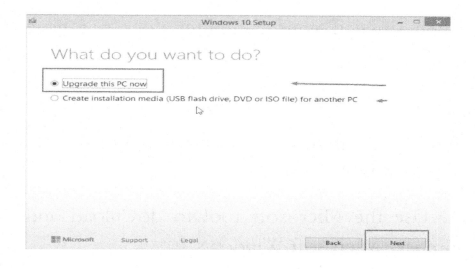

If you do not purchase an activated copy of Windows 10, you will have to instal it separately. You could prefer to do system clean installation of Windows 10 instead. Installing Windows 10 is not that hard as Windows 7, however there is one issue.

Typically, the Windows 10 licence is provided on a DVD. Installing the virus programme is as easy as inserting a disc.

It is essential to instal Windows 10 from the

flash drive if your computer does not have CD rom.

There are a number of different ways to create a bootable flash drive.

1. Use the Microsoft tool to download and prepare Microsoft Windows 10

No installation is necessary: this process is very simple. Then, you just download it and move it to your flash drive.

First, you need to launch the Windows 10 Installation Media Creation Tool.

Second, Choose the media type and press next.

This is the only correct method. Use the

Windows 7 USB/DVD Download Tool if you already have a Windows Vista ISO image.

Like in the picture above, you should select the architecture, edition and language. Click next.

Finally, choose USB flash drive and click Next.

Next, you will click finish. Your installation disc has been installed. After connecting USB device to the computer, restart the computer. If things have been set up correctly, Windows 10 installation begins automatically.

Click the blue button and follow the instructions.

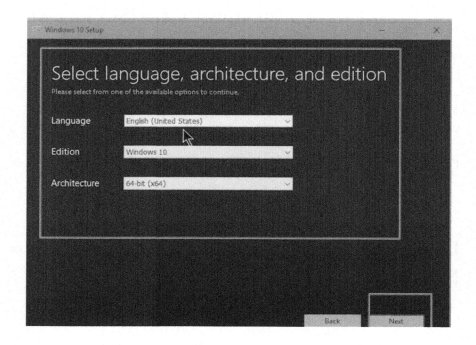

Upgrading your computer.

If you want to instal a new operating system on your computer, you have to go into the BIOS SETUP and select the boot from a DVD or flash drive (depending on the type of media from which you will instal Windows).

8

The key combinations on laptops may vary from computer to computer.

You must press a particular key during the installation process (ICT-initial computer testing, which is performed immediately after turning on the PC).

It appears that the most used method to enter the BIOS is to use Delete key. It is the least used F1, F2 keys.

There are two ways to find out the BIOS key:.

1. From the chassis to motherboard.

2. Based on what the prompt on the screen currently indicates This means that the message "Press Delete to enter Setup" is displayed, then Delete must be pressed to enter the BIOS. Hold down the key after the prompt appears on the screen.

On a regular basis, various prompts are

displayed on the computer display screen.

3. The word prompt can sometimes be missing on the screen. Then you need to press the key several times after the first image is displayed on the screen.

Attention. If the prompt does not appear on the screen at all, enter the BIOS according to the following key combinations:.

1. F1,

2. F2,

3. F3,

4. Delete;

5. F10,

6. F11,

7. F12;

8. Ctrl + Alt + S;

9. Ctrl + Shift + S;

10. Ctrl + Alt + Del;

11. Ctrl + Alt + Esc;

12. ESC.

Sometimes other keys can also be found on the scene.

1. Ins.

2. Or-"Or-"

3. Ctrl+;.

4. Ctrl + Shift + Esc;.

5. Ctrl + Alt + Shift;.

6. Ctrl+Alt+Del;.

7. Press Ctrl+S.

8. Ctrl + Space;

9. Ctrl + Shift + Alt + Del.

After you see the language selection menu, click the desired language. English will be selected automatically and you are just required to click next. If you have ever installed previous versions of Windows (versions 7 and 8), then this window will appear to be very familiar.

Then, you will see a prompt with an option instal.

Then you need to input the product code.

After accepting the terms of the licence, you have to choose the type of equipment you will use.

Since we are changing the operating system from the old computer, you will need to activate Windows only.

In the next step, you need to choose the drive on which you will instal Windows 10.

Hmmm... For normal operation of Windows 10, your computer must have at least 1 GB of free disc space. The "minimum needed" according to Microsoft are 20 GB and 16 GB. Microsoft is definitely not perfect. Microsoft Windows 64-bit comes in a matter of hours after installation. With 32-bit and operating system, work is fast, graphics is beautiful, and so on. Only 6 gigabytes.

The installation process should begin. After the thing installed automatically, your computer will reboot. This can take from several minutes to several hours. On SSDs, there is no lengthy wait for installation.

In the next screen, you will see a black screen with the Windows 10 logo, and then you will see a system recovery process.

At this point, the installer will offer to you set

some parameters. After installation, you can still change all the parameters before clicking the Click here and Click here to set the settings.

Windows 10 will then search for critical updates from Microsoft's own servers, but can also download the updates directly from the Microsoft servers if the user is connected to the internet.

Create your Microsoft account here.

The next step to setting up a computer is to create a user account. If you have an account, just log in to your account. The user does not have to create a Microsoft account during the Windows 10 installation process. If you want to use certain functions of Microsoft, you will have to create a Microsoft account.

All right, so please enter your username and password. It is essential to set a password for safeguarding your computer. Having even the simplest password protects data being encrypted with system tools. For encryption with EFS, you should set the password to be sure.

The user will wait while the system preconfigures applications.

Once your network settings are configured, your Personal Computer will detect other computers and devices on your network. If your network includes other computers, then select yes; otherwise choose no.

That's really all. You will see the improved

specifications of the upcoming version of Windows.

Chapter 2: The Start Menu and the Settings Menu. Here are the basic things one should have.

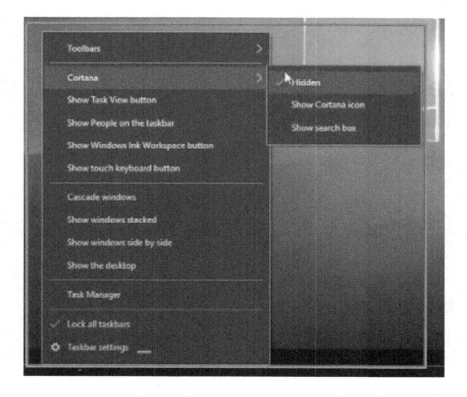

Windows Taskbar.

Start Menu button is on the bottom left corner of the desktop screen. With this button, we will access programmes and applications in our personal computer. They will be represented as icons on the left of the menu and "glance" on the right.

Let us start by examining the controls on the left side. Repeat them...

- SEARCH.

- The 'Shutdown and Reboot' command under the Start menu.

- This is the main Settings screen, above the Reboot button.

The most popular and newest icons.

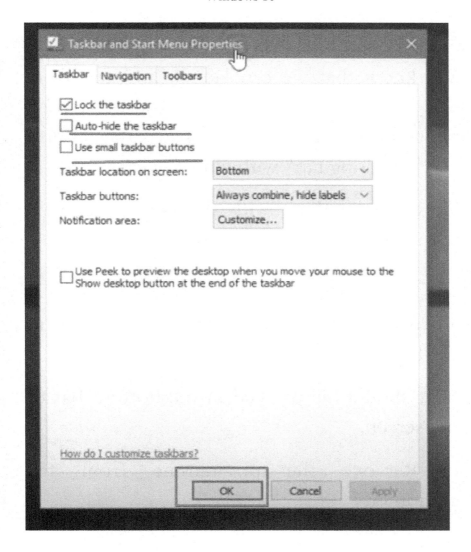

Let us start from basic things and explain in detail.

Windows does this so it's easier for us to find

things.

We know that we can launch any app from this list by clicking the left button or "tap" if we work in a tablet. Also, what is the result if you use "long tap" with your finger?

This can be done with the help of context menu. This menu can also be used to:.

a. Program the frequently used items (Pin to the home screen).

b. It should be installed in the bottom bar of the screen.

c. Remove the programme from the computer.

d. Run as administrator (we have to do this very rarely - and only with old programmes adapted for Windows 7).

e. To run the programme, open the folder where this programme is stored.

Not only with the Frequently Used and Recently Added menus but also any icons in the Column headers.

The first two points should be considered. The first thing you should do is to put the icons for the applications you need on the Taskbar. In that way, you can run programmes simply without opening start menu.

It is possible to adjust the size of your icons in this way. You can quickly find the programme you need without having to open the Start menu - just type part of its name into the Search option in the bottom left corner of the screen.

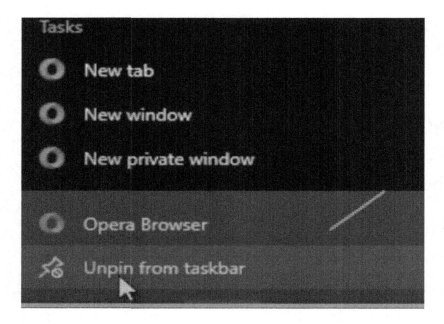

List of apps.

The icons of all of the programmes installed on the computer have been arranged in alphabetical order. There's such a huge list. Wow. Now imagine that there is word processing application called Word that is last in the Start menu. There will not be any need to flip through the list as you can simply click or tap the table of contents.

Launch Application (Tile Panel)

"Tiles" of new universal Windows applications are placed in the left side of the screen (in Tablet mode, this area is called the Start screen, and it really takes up the entire screen).

Live tiles enable you to know the minute changes in stocks and currencies in the system.

You can drag tiles from one location to another, and add them to the Taskbar at the bottom of the screen (for this you need to call the Context menu with a right-click). The unnecessary tiles can be removed by right-clicking it and selecting "Delete" instead of dragging and dropping it to the right.

Tiles can be combined into folders - just drag one onto another with the mouse.

Windows suggests displaying multiple tiles differently by putting them in groups. There will be two or more of them at first but because of Windows Metro on-boarding, they will become active after that.

In Windows Vista, you can place the tile of any application from the All Applications menu on the Start menu - just click its icon with the right mouse button, and select the Pin command on the Start menu. In the same way, you can send the desired icon to the Taskbar, or "taskbar" at the bottom of the screen - usually those applications that we always want to have been given this honour. And also an extra icon that you don't need can be removed from the Home screen (or the Taskbar).

Launch System Settings.

The Start menu can be configured by modifying the Start options. In the start menu, we select customization next to start.

However, you can disable folders that are Frequently Used, Recently Installed, & Recommended Applications under the Start menu (this should be done first). Start menu settings allow you to full screen the Home screen and select the list of folders that will be displayed on the Start menu tile.

Open the context menu.

We already know about the context menu. It appears if you click the button with the mouse button (in tablet mode, it is called a long press). We have already mentioned on the list of icons in the applications menu. You will also see what happens when you right-click on the Start button itself.

It's nice to have many tools within the context menu of this button. This is an administrator setting menu

From here, you can open and manipulate your Windows Explorer window, the Power Manager, the Task Manager, the Windows Firewall, the Control Panel ... The toolset will include PowerShell commands and a device manager that can collect information from hardware in your PC. It should be remembered that fast is the most convenient way to access most of them here . (although there are other ways to call each tool).

1. As an example, in order to turn off the computer through the Start menu, we need three clicks of the mouse, and through the Context menu, we only need to click it with one click, not three.

2. Firstly, we need to click the Start button, then the Settings button, and then the Applications option. This can be accomplished through context menu of the Start button.

3. You can find Disk Management nowhere in Windows. You can only find this kind of option in the context menu of the Start button. This technology is dangerous in inexperienced hands.

The settings menu.

Therefore, the most necessary tools for configuring the system are available in Settings menu and we'll have to familiarise ourselves with all controls there. Before Windows 10, all the control operations for setting up the computer were carried out via the Control Panel, which was saved into

Windows 10, but was pushed into the background because it is not appropriate for touch operations and is also too busy for use.

Click Start > Control Panel > Programs > Turn Windows features on or off. I believe immediately pinning the touch icon on the taskbar is best. This is known:.

First of all, open the command prompt window.

Next, right-click the gear icon that appears to the left;.

Third Phase: Select "Pin to taskbar" item.

Access Menus.

Of course, familiarity with Windows 10 would enable for a much better experience using the built-in search engine. We will likely use this in tablet mode and in classic mode. The

Search menu allows you to search Internet and files on your computer, . (you can search by documents, programme names and settings, even for pictures and music).

Here is an example. In order to reach the Backup Settings in the Desktop mode, you must first right-click on the left of the screen. Go to the System and security section, click on the Support Center button and go to the System Restore function. Windows now has a global Search function that provides access to any type of document, programme or configuration tool.

By default, a single list of topics related to what is being searched - photos, music, documents, system settings and even email. But you can always sort a particular category - a link with icons below. Nothing is unclear.

Secondly, it can be dragged with the mouse pointer to any part of the panel or any part of the Search menu.

The search box menu item is shown as an icon next to the Start button in Windows 10. In my opinion, switching to Line Mode would be more convenient. You can easily change an option by using the context menu (right-click, Search next Show search field).

Chapter 3: Classical applications

Applications in Windows 10 are modified in manner similar to Microsoft product named Metro. The late entries are distinguished by a more functional and attractive interfaces, but they are actually very basic applications.

New applications are launched in wided mode of Windows due to the return of the classic desktop. Many internet users have the capability to switch to full-screen mode. It switches to work with it when it is working in tablet mode.

We will not consider Windows desktop programmes They are known from previous versions of Windows. You can start standard Windows 10 applications through the start menu or the All Apps menu.

You can instal extra applications, and you can use the Store application.

Applications:

1. Calendar is an easy-to-use scheduling application.

2. Email is an electronic mail programme. It is too simple. For corporate emails, Outlook is a good programme.

3. OneNote - creates notes.

4. With this app, you can find out news without being bored.

5. Weather is always at hand with the Internet.

6. Finance provides news and information about the financial information in the world.

7. Xbox - helps you connect your computer with your Xbox game console.

8. OneDrive is like an OS for mobile devices. The user will be able to set alarms.

9. Calculator - this is a modern machine for calculating.

9. Maps - maps and GPS navigation devices on your computers.

11 Camera - you can work with a camera on

your computer.

13. Sports news

13 A programme that enables you to draw three-dimensional pictures.

All of these applications are simple and anyone can figure them out. Therefore, we're only going to consider the most interesting applications of IT.

The Holidays.

The Calendar app can integrate with various calendar services. This means that if you keep a day planner on your Android handset, it will be able to connect to the Google service and obtain your agenda. Of course, there will be similar changes across the country.

Now we can see how to use the calendar on your android phone. When the account is created you will be able to launch the application. Recorded At last, you should select a type of account - Google! In the form that appears, enter the email address and password in the box, then scroll down and give permission for this application to use your Google account by clicking the Allow button.

At that time, you should begin working on your calendar. On the left you see a month calendar that you will need to use. As can be seen from Figure 5 12.7, we have two calendars - a calendar stored in Microsoft account and one stored in Gmail.

At the top of the screen is a row of four buttons - Day, Workweek, Week, Today. Click the Add Event button to add a new event. Please enter the event title, description, start time, and finish time. When adding an event to your diary, make sure you are adding it to the right calendar. The application is being downloaded to the Microsoft account.

Click "Save and Close" to record this event on your calendar.

Calculator.

The Calculator is a built-in feature that comes with all versions of Windows 10. The probability that is mentioned or the user is essential. Most Windows users face a problem in finding a programme very easily in the new Windows.

The calculator is now located in the lower-right corner. Once it was in the standard Start menu item, but now has its own programme programme. The calculator sometimes may not appear at the intended location. Now, use the search field on the website.

You can still find the calculator after going at this path: your system drive, C:, then windows, then system32, then calc.exe. This software isn't just for home users, that's for sure.

If you checked Start menu and tried to search in the folder specified, and the search didn't turn up anything, then most likely your calculator was removed from the folder. It's just a silly mistake, don't worry about it. To connect windows 10 to bluetooth, click here. In the application installation search for "Calculator" and you will see a list of apps you can instal on your PC.

If the calculator is not starting, you need to try the following:

If looking for the Applications and Features section, look in Start Settings-System-Applications and Features.

2) Among the ideas mentioned, look at "Calculator". Under the advanced options, you should visit the Contact form item.

Press the "Reset" button.

Now that that is done, click on Calculator again.

Chapter 4: Excel: An Overview.

The Microsoft Store is a location where you can download free software. You don't need to be a dinosaur to use it. We have always learned that from the same Google Play and AppStore you can import and update games for free. They can provide paying apps, so you do not have to use them.

In Windows 8, though, Metro apps form a different type of applications. The business introduced full screen mode apps that were designed for Smartphones, tablets and personal computers. Applications are being downloaded from the Microsoft Marketplace and from the Apple App Store. In Windows 10, several programmes in this class operate in windowed mode. From the point of view of the consumer, all implementations are the same. The primary distinction between desktop applications built using installers and those installed by using Windows Store is that:

Advantages with Microsoft Shops in Singapore.

Xbox Lounge has one positive - it is connected to your Microsoft account. This software will handle installation of all programmes. All the details and knowledge that is contained in your account.

To sum up, reinstalling Windows may become a very boring process. You will be told of the latest programmes that are installed in your account. If you downloaded applications, so you won't need to order them again.

Download apps.

Launch the Microsoft store programme (in Windows 10, it is simply called the Store). Then search for the programme you want to instal. Today there are many apps to pick from and they are all fairly appealing.

As a consequence, the view indicates that programme Calculator + HD is chosen. To trigger the instalment, press the "Get" icon. If you do not have a Microsoft account, then register for one.

The shop will seem to be mundane and harmless but it will try to trick the users into using a Microsoft account. Opt out at this time.

That's it. The programme continues to download. The method of installing the software is reflected in the Store window.

When you instal shop, you can see an announcement in the store pane. To gain access to this programme, you must press the Open button or start the application from the main menu.

View an installed programme.

You need to press on the library icon and choose My Library. You can see a number of programmes that you recently installed, but which haven't been installed.

Applications that were previously installed but which were not installed on this device are marked by a tiny red arrow downwards. You should import and update the software on the current machine.

There is no uninstall for programme. It is really commendable because they take up very little room. In previous models, there was an erase option but in Windows 10, it was disabled.

Chapter 5: Taskbar.

There are icons on the Windows taskbar that are often needed.

- Check the website;

- Internet Edge Browser

- Email services.

- Microsoft Shop, from which we instal other software.

You will drag the icon of any application into the Panel with your mouse.

You may place Dock icon on Taskbar by following these steps: You will more quickly click on the command put at the taskbar. Look at the image above.

You may even delete the presence of a shortcut from the Taskbar (right clicking on the icon is the Remove programme from taskbar command). See the screenshot below.

You will navigate the already running programmes via the application bar. It is worth mentioning that miniaturised icons can pop up in the Taskbar while the software is working. Alternatively, windows could be displayed if several windows are opened. See the screenshot below.

For most applications in the Taskbar, as well as for similar functions, there are tiny control panels that are now accessible as thumbnails. You should, for example, address an incoming message, pause an album ...

To trigger the window you referred to, as you point to it with the mouse button, all other open windows for a limited period will become translucent. But before you place your cursor on top of this region.

The taskbar settings are contained in Settings, Framework, Taskbar. The installation may be attached both at the bottom and at the top of the screen and maximise the amount of icons on the taskbar.

Chapter 6: Trey

The Trebuchet in Windows 10 works nearly similarly to the Trebuchet from Windows 7. People may use Trey for viewing alerts of device activity and software (network setting, sound settings, battery level of the portable device). Trey is positioned at the bottom right-hand corner of the screen.

These are several common symbols used by

Trey in his paintings.

1. Menu of fast contact

2. OneDrive.

3. Keyboard switch Punto Switcher

4. Computer connection by cable or a wifi connection

5. Clock and schedule by calendar.

6. Notification center.

Any icons can be dragged into the main panel in the same way by only pressing the "pointer". Only note not to drag windows icons from the Screen to the Notification Pad, it isn't for that.

When you press on the clock on the right, you can open the Calendar and time zone settings (if you need something for some reason). And be alert to threat.

We should bear in mind that closing the computer screen will reduce windows into tiny icons in the taskbar.

These configurations can be configured in the menu "Personalization > Taskbar." You may activate or disable the icons of any programmes that claim to own this sandy beach in the notification area section.

Alerts.

Trays are one of the characteristics of the machine Trey and one of the distinctive features of Windows 10. It creates a new functional tool called Notification Hub.

Here are notifications telling you what you may or may not have overlooked. Email message and missing calls alerts can appear here, even those on Android phones (I remind you that you need to instal Cortana voice assistant on your phone or tablet).

You can clear all notifications at once using the button on the top right corner of the screen.

Please. The most relevant alerts would appear at the bottom right of the page.

Chapter 7: Windows 10 on Your Laptop.

Individualization.

After opening Windows, it is normal to see the calendar and toolbars on the desktop.

Windows is able to be shaped to fit your preferences.

The Microsoft's personalization is known by the word "personalization," because it's all about the customising functions.

Both modifications regarding Desktop interface can be located in Options - Personalization Menu.

Let us dig through some cases.

One we are conscious - via the Start menu settings icon.

In addition, you can search Personalization in Google (in this case, you will be taken to the corresponding section of the old Control Panel - there are a few more settings).

Some people use strategies such as right-clicking on the desktop, then pick "personalization."

Adjust the style.

On-screen "themes" encourage you to adjust the look and colour of all components of Windows at once. Many topics use many "wallpapers" that cover one another regularly.

Of course, every book of topics is not adequate. Fortunately, you can now browse new ones (free!) at the Microsoft website by selecting the other topics connection in the shop. This website hosts a range of interesting material coupled with images and videos from all over the globe.

Adjust the picture, please.

The number of users who do not want to play with themes is growing. This can be achieved by way of wallpaper models as each of them can contain a number of the associated themes. If you like to use your own image as a backdrop, no issue with that!

Right-click on the desktop computer and select a background.

You may use the blank canvas to set a frame, wallpaper or any image for the desktop (for example, Images).

By clicking on Browse in the Pick toolbar, you can choose any picture from any folder as the backdrop - including from the Screen on which you copied the photo from the Internet.

Defections. You will send an email directly to your screen by putting an image there ... For any secret file: Right-click and pick Set Desktop as Background picture....

Change the paint scheme.

The next menu object, "Personalization", provides one with the option to change colours.

We do have our favourite colours. It is impossible to avoid hue "co-dependency" - we can turn Windows from appearing pale into our desired colour easily enough. If they are on your own stylistic taste, you will get uncomfortable with their presentation. You don't need to think about colour matching - there are loads of colour schemes in the software. There is another form of colour selection called automated colour selection which would be implemented based on the background pictures. So, when using this menu, you can select one of two interface models - Light Window (Installed by default) or Dark Window.

You may choose to select various colours in the title bars and in the Start menu to support the consumer who is having cognitive disabilities.

This is anything which can differ from one screen to another.

Does this bother you? Secondly, we need to name the Edit menu and pick the Settings command.

There should be an alternative to resize the text on the option menu. Ths same approach may be used when renaming files or services.

Here we increase the size of all things on the screen: the buttons, the captions on the them, and the window names.

Look through the microscope.

For those with poor vision, the Video Magnifier is used in both models of Windows to allow you to expand pictures or photographs in different windows (for example, Internet pages in a browser). To locate this programme, click here or use the Search at the bottom of the list (just type the word Loop).

Pressing the Windows key plus the plus sign, and Windows key plus the minus sign would enable you to zoom through the screen.

When interacting on a touch screen (for example, an iPad), you would be able to:.

Users are able to "zoom in and out" with a "tap" at the corners of the device.

Tap the side of the screen and switch the cursor around.

You can turn off Magnifier mode by pressing the cross at the upper right of the device.

Browser Virtualization.

You may control virtual desktops by clicking the Display Mode button 'n' on the Taskbar, or by pressing the Windows key + the N or C buttons.

Connect application windows to a virtual table using the context menu button (right-click).

It is also possible to be managed using these hotkey variations on PCs:

Windows + F + D - open new desktop;.

Desktop + F + n - delete the present desktop;

Click the Windows + F keys - flipping between desktops.

Chapter 8: Personal directories.

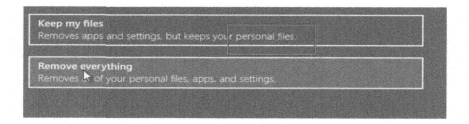

Personal files.

We must still think of Personal Folders, of course. Both personal folders are also available from the Start menu of Windows.

The service should be ordered to allow more comfort to the customers. On the Taskbar, these four types show as Documented TV, Recorded Movies, Recorded Music, and

Recorded Records.

Personal Directories offer you some valuable benefits as all providers have a specific connection with them. All files stored in Personal Directories are indexed, which means any file stored there can be searched through search by name and material. This applies to records that can be traced using keywords or phrases.

Both applications are aware of this. For example, if you transfer photographs from your mobile to your machine, Windows would ask you to use Photos to store them.

Chapter 9: preserving and diagnosing and protection of your PC.

In this part, we look at how to give your machine full protection and also how to avoid crashes.

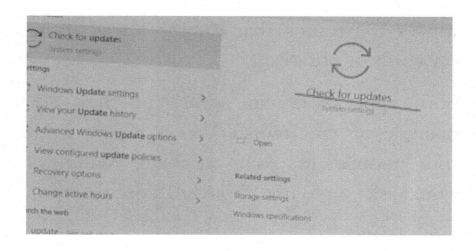

Microsoft Update.

This is the most critical protection law that they need to submit patches. Most enhancements concern protection protections. To enforce this function, you must go to the Upgrade tab, and select the Protection tab.

Unlike prior iterations, Windows 10 includes an Upgrade Center that can simultaneously search for and instal all changes.

However, certain aspects of the functionality may be customised. They are: press "Additional options".

By checking the "subscription" box, you'll enable Microsoft to automatically upgrade Workplace, Internet Explorer, and other items on your device. In addition, you would have a chance to download fresh Windows assemblies because you are an insider in this scheme. You would be able to carry out functions until they are usable in normal computer users. The slider on the side of the dialogue window will give you the choice of selecting between the slow and quick notifications (all new updates, including ones with functions that are not yet fully debugged).

Windows Defender.

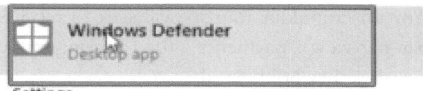

A few people assume that viruses can trigger data loss without any difficulty. Or, extracts the passwords and credit card numbers from a device. However, ransomware is just the tip of the iceberg.

The computer viruses carry on a malevolent function by targeting computers of major corporations during irregular times.

Any unscrupulous tourists will seek to receive pay-per-view payments for pornographic websites they hold illegal.

As you suspect, this is yet another cookie poisoning strike.

In addition, this operating system would also prompt the consumer to automatically transfer money from his or her wallet or account to the phones. These applications also claim to be warnings, warning you that your operating system is no longer legal.

In several cases this is the most common block because of the different purpose. Other viruses function by encrypting all the data on the hard disc. There is less danger from ransomware that utilises the device. One of the drawbacks of cryptocurrencies being that they may slow down the economic processes of different countries.

If we want it or not, we would need some sort of antivirus to defend the PCs from viruses.

Security and ease.

In such a way, you can reach the core by right-clicking on an icon in the device tray (the lower right corner). You may also access the Windows Defender settings pane from the Settings Menu.

The requisite security points are already allowed by now, you don't need to worry about it anymore. Since such functionality was included into the latest edition of Windows 10, it could disappoint some users. It is important to delete viruses which can't be handled while the device is operating. In order to shield yourself from computer viruses and spyware, you should press the "Advanced Scan" button and then pick "Windows Standalone Defender Scan." The Registry search will begin after the device finishes rebooting after the Windows shell takes its position in the running memory.

As well as being secured by the antivirus framework, the operating system is often protected from running unauthorised applications (User Account Control). One of the tasks of UAC is to cut off non-customized and unnecessary programmes you have to launch.

UAC is very irritating to the extreme, and thus, beginners automatically opt to uninstall it. This is pretty clear ... However, are protection precautions such as this anything that a fantastic machine can forego? You should be confident that without authorization, a programme would not be activated on your device.

If during installation of the programme, this window appears and you are completely sure that the software does not risk any potential hazard, click on the Information tab.

Classic viruses in recent years are less violent. Besides, there is an exception to troubles: "advertising."

Unchecky will partly guard you from downloading applications that you don't want to instal.

In this way, device hijacking can be prevented by downloading reasonable antivirus apps. A harmful "windows activator" downloads a marketing programme that cannot be cleaned away with normal cleaning equipment.

One click on the advertisements will trigger them to show up in the browser. Since restarting the window, the web will also feature a pop-up advert any time.

Both exterior and within-frame commercials could be managed through these features:

Download AdwCleaner

SuperAntiSpyware is an outstanding anti-spyware.

This is the only way out and "restore points" is the only way to return a structure to the former state of that system". In the event of system failure, absolutely rest the system.

Chapter 10: How to Set up Remote Access to Your Device

If you are new to utilising this operating system, so you would possibly need some assistance. Windows 10 provides an outstanding functionality that helps users to attach to the home machine from the sofa and "fix" issues.

There are several programmes, such as Remote Desktop Link, that make you remotely login to your personal computer and function from there.

All of these applications is available in Windows 10 - it is named Fast Assist, and you can reach it, as always, by pressing 'Windows + X' on the keyboard.

So now we need to consider what we can do - to support each other or to ask others for help. In this alternative, we begin with the previous option. Tap on the icon to vote.

This software will create a six-digit authentication code for you, which you will give to your assistant to sign. Upon receipt of this code, your assistant can open Support and then click on the Get Help icon, and input the code you submitted.

The next move is that your machine can immediately connect to the target device and you can take some action: pass any data to the remote computer, etc.

Even if it has simple architecture, Fast Support is not anything super-complete in the marketplace.

Chapter 11: Secret ties

Windows do not want to screen regular apps since trusting so many applications to newcomers is risky. Yes, they aren't important at all. However, with the right keywords, it is simple to study secret utilities.

The most critical of these tools:

- Disk Cleaner is a really successful programme. Personally, I suggest you substitute a different CCleaner deletion utility.

Defrag to get rid of imaged data. Windows often disburses fragmented across surface of hard disc and impacts output while multitasking. Although defragmentation is not as important as before, Windows progressively tracks the order, so it is advised to defragment manually every few months. This does not refer to solid state drives (SSDs)

- •Configuration. Fine-grained boot regulation here to avoid severe boot entry.

- Machine performance. A detailed report on hardware and software structures on the device to be stored as a text paper.

- Method to stimulate memory. Check RAM modules for potential physical faults. You need to restart the machine.

- Computerization. One of the most effective software to customise the framework is PresentationEngine However, Disk Maintenance is most important aspect here. With UltraISO we can conveniently format any drive, build several logical partitions and handle our partition discs.

Remember. A brand new disc must be designed for one of these activities.

- Useful Programs. Monitoring machine operating system facilities. At one point, it was trendy to switch off the "Useless" programmes on the device (for example, Fax, support for touch screens, and sometimes even the System Restore service).

Windows has a "PowerShell" command line, where you can pick "Run as Administrator" from the context menu of the Start button, or by tapping PowerShell into the search bar.

Programs that could be called from the command line mode or from the Run menu:

- appwiz.cpl - Removing programs;

- charmap - Character table;

- calc - Calculator;

- cleanmgr - cleaning disks utility ;

- chkdsk - checking disks utility;

- cmd - Command line;

- control - control panel;

- control admintools - Administration;

- compmgmt.msc - Computer Management;

- control folders - Folder properties;

- control desktop - Screen Settings / Personalization;

- control keyboard - properties of keyboard;

- control mouse - Mouse properties;

- control fonts - Fonts;

- control schedtasks - Task Scheduler;

- control printers - pinters and devices;

- desk.cpl - Screen resolution;

- devmgmt.msc - Device Manager;

- dfrgui - Disk Defragmenter;

- dxdiag - DirectX Diagnostic Tools;

- firefox - Firefox ;

- eventvwr.msc - events viewer;

- diskmgmt.msc - Disk Management;

- explorer - Windows Explorer;

- iexplore - Internet Explorer;

- firewall.cpl - Windows Firewall;

- logoff - Log out of the Windows user account;

- inetcpl.cpl - Internet Explorer properties;

- main.cpl - Mouse Properties;

- magnify - Magnifier (magnifying glass);

- mmsys.cpl - Sound settings;

- migwiz -Transfer Tool;

- msconfig - system configuration;

- mrt - malware removal tool;

- mspaint - Graphic Paint editor;

- msinfo32 - System Information;

- osk - On-screen keyboard;

- ncpa.cpl - Network connections;

- notepad - Notepad;

- powercfg.cpl - Power supply;

- perfmon - System Monitor;

- rrr -Reg Organizer Quick launch ;

- prs - recording problems reproduction tool;

- regedit - Registry Editor;

- shutdown - Windows Shutdown;

- timedate.cpl - Date and Time Settings;

- sysdm.cpl - System Properties;

- askmgr - Task Manager;

syskey - Protection of the database of Windows accounts;

- utilman - Accessibility Center;

- verifier - checking drivers manager;

- winver - Windows version;

- wab - Address Book;

- wmplayer - Media Player;

- wscui.cpl - the Center of Support .

- write - Editor for Wordpad;

Conclusion

Our book is suitable for both beginners and those who want to learn more about Windows 10's advances. We have shared important pieces of information including from basic to advanced chips.

I hope, that you really enjoyed reading my book.

Thanks for buying the book anyway!

Made in the USA
Monee, IL
05 May 2021